BLOG LOVE

Chris Moore

STARTER
LEVEL

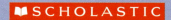

Material written by: Chris Moore
Commissioning Editor: Jacquie Bloese
Editor: Fiona Beddall
Cover design: Dawn Wilson
Designer: Dawn Wilson
Picture research: Emma Bree
Photo credits:
Page 4: Photodisc; Image 100.
Page 5: Image 100.
Page 24: Hemera; IT Stock Free; A. Segre, P. Svarc/Alamy.
Page 25: Bananastock/Punchstock; Creatas; Big Cheese/Alamy; D. Ardian/Getty Images.
Page 26: Imagestate.
Illustrations: Katie Mac

No part of this publication may be reproduced in whole or in part, or stored in a retrieval system, or transmitted in any form or by any means, electronic, mechanical, photocopying, recording or otherwise, without written permission of the publisher. For information regarding permission write to:

Mary Glasgow Magazines (Scholastic Ltd.)
Euston House
24 Eversholt Street
London
NW1 1DB

© Chris Moore 2006
All rights reserved.

Printed in Malaysia

Reprinted in 2007, 2009, 2010, 2012, 2013, 2014, 2015, 2016 and 2017

CONTENTS

	PAGE
Blog Love	4–23
People and places	4
Chapter 1: Write to me!	6
Chapter 2: Slow or fast?	11
Chapter 3: Slow Boy in London	17
Fact Files	24–27
The web world	24
Lonely in London	26
Self-Study Activities	28–30
New Words!	32

PEOPLE AND PLACES

BLOG LOVE

JUNKO NAGAI

Junko is 17. She's from Japan. She's learning English in London, but she has no friends there. She starts a blog and meets a boy on it.

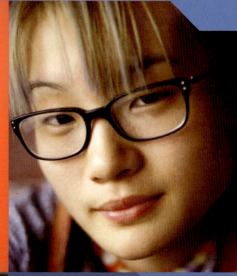

SONYA SIPOVNA

Sonya is learning English at Junko's language school. She's from Slovakia. She likes boys and clothes and motorbikes.

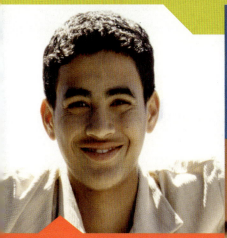

SILVIO ROSSI

Silvio is learning English too. He's Italian. He likes Sonya.

JEFF SILK

Jeff is the owner of the Double Decker Internet Café. He has a big motorbike. He loves girls with glasses.

SLOW BOY

PLACES

St Martin's Language School: Junko, Sonya and Silvio learn English here.
The Double Decker Internet Café: Junko writes her blog here.

BLOG LOVE

CHAPTER 1: Write to me!

Monday July 11th – 15.39 **by Junko**

I'm writing this blog in the Double Decker Internet Café in London. The café is in a tall, old, red London bus next to my language school. I love it. It's very British.

I'm from Tokyo but I'm living in the UK for three months. I'm learning English here. My name's Junko. This is me. I've got black hair, dark eyes, glasses and a big smile.

Please write to me at my blog.
Goodbye for today!

0 messages

Thursday July 14th – 15.42　　　　　　　　　　**by Junko**

Internet, I'm telling you about my life in England because you're my only friend here.

I'm living with Mr and Mrs Lacey. Mr Lacey works in a cinema. Mrs Lacey is a policewoman. They always ask me the same thing: 'How are you today?'
'OK,' I answer.
I ask about London, but Mr Lacey says, 'Let's talk this evening. I'm going to work now. Goodbye, Junko. Have a good day!'

In the evenings, I say hello to Mr Lacey. But he says, 'I'm very, very tired. A terrible day at the cinema! I'm going to bed now. Goodnight.'

Sometimes I feel very lonely.

0 messages

Tuesday July 19th – 15.56　　　　　　　　　　**by Junko**

Hello, Internet, you're not my only friend in England!!

In the street next to the internet café, a girl says to me, 'You're Japanese. I know your face from language school. I'm Sonya. I'm from Slovakia. What's your name?'
'I'm Junko. Junko Nagai.'

Sonya has dark hair and green eyes and expensive jeans. 'I love Japan!' she says.

'Do you know Japan?' I ask.
'I know Japanese mobile phones. They're my favourite.'
We look at my mobile.

'That's cool. I want one too. Have you got a boyfriend in England?'
'No.'
'Which boys do you like in school? I like Silvio. His clothes are from Sergio Tacchini. I like English boys too. They drive cool cars and they've got great mobile phones. Have you got a car? My father's buying me a Passat, but I want a Mercedes ...'

0 messages

Thursday July 21st – 15.15   by Junko

50 of us from school are in Oxford. It's an hour from London on the train.

Oxford is famous because lots of students live here. Sonya is very happy. 'Oxford students have lots of money,' she says.

But I'm not happy. Sonya isn't talking to me today. She's always with Silvio.

Silvio's from Italy. He has short, dark hair, exciting eyes and clothes from Sergio Tacchini. His English is very bad.

We go to some important buildings in Oxford. But Sonya doesn't look at the buildings. She only looks at Silvio, and Silvio only looks at her. They don't want me there with them.

I'm writing this in an internet café in Oxford. Are Sonya and Silvio in love? What can I say to them on the train to London?

0 messages

Saturday July 23rd – 10.46 **by Junko**

It's Saturday morning. Sonya is shopping in Oxford Street with Silvio, not with me. The Laceys are working. Saturday is a big day at the cinema, and at the police station.

There are only two people in the Double Decker Internet Café, me and the owner – and 30 computers. The owner's name is Jeff. He's old – maybe 25. He has brown hair and blue eyes. Maybe he reads this blog.

He asks me, 'Do you like my café?'
'Very, very much,' I say.
He smiles and touches my hand.

0 messages

CHAPTER 2: Slow or fast?

Thursday July 28th – 15.41   **by Junko**

Jeff is watching me a lot today. I look up, and he smiles at me. I look back at my computer. I look up again. Again Jeff is looking at me. Does he like me? Maybe we can be friends.

Oh, oh, oh! I've got a message on my blog. It's from Slow Boy. Thank you, Slow Boy!

1 message

> **Thursday July 28th – 10.18**   **by Slow Boy**
>
> Hello, Japanese Junko. I like reading your blog. I'm learning Japanese in Tokyo. I'm in Japan for six months. I've got one or two friends here. But they're new friends, not my old friends back in London.
>
> I like Japan, but sometimes I feel lonely too. Write to me! I'm waiting for a message from you.

Don't be sad, Slow Boy. We can be blog friends. We can laugh about our problems.

Tuesday August 2nd – 15.39   **by Junko**

In the school café, Sonya is looking at Andreas's mobile. 'That's a cool mobile!' she says.

He answers, 'I'm buying a Suzuki motorbike too. I have the money.'
Sonya looks into Andreas's eyes and smiles.
'Do you like my new green T-shirt? It's from Top Shop in Oxford Street.'
'It's the colour of your eyes, Sonya.'
'Do you like my jeans?'
'Yes, and I like the person in the jeans too.'
'They're from Gap,' she smiles.

Where's Silvio? There! He's looking at Sonya, but Sonya isn't looking at him. Maybe she isn't in love with him today.

1 message

Tuesday August 2nd – 10.20   **by Slow Boy**

```
There's a girl here in Tokyo. We take the same
bus every day. But she's very shy. How can I be
friends with her?
```

Be very polite, Slow Boy. Open the door of the bus for her. Japanese girls like polite boys.

Friday August 5th – 15.44   **by Junko**

Silvio is very quiet at school today. He's sad because of Sonya. She sits next to Andreas now. Andreas's family has lots of money.

Andreas and Silvio and Sonya never talk to me. But I'm not sad. I've got a blog friend.

In the internet café there's a hand on my back. I look up. It's Jeff, the owner. I go to a different window on the computer. He can't see my blog now.

'Do you want a drink, baby?'
'OK.'
'Let's go to the West End on my motorbike.'
How can I say no? Jeff is my first friend in England.
'Motorbike? Now?' I say.
'Honda. Japanese. Quiet and no problems. Come on!'

We go down the street very fast. Next to the language school, Sonya and Andreas are talking. They see me and smile.

Jeff says, 'Friends?'
'Maybe. I don't know,' I answer.
'I see. Let's go back. We can say hello to them.'
'Can I go home now?'
'OK, baby, no problem.'

0 messages

Monday August 8th – 15.40　　　　　　　　**by Junko**

'Who's the boy, Junko?' Sonya smiles at me. 'He's got a great motorbike.'
'His name's Jeff.'
'A Honda,' Andreas says. 'Not bad. But I'm buying a Suzuki 600. It's expensive and fast.'
'How do you know Jeff?' Sonya asks.
'He's a … a friend,' I answer.
'Oh?' Sonya and Andreas say.

Silvio is listening but he doesn't smile. He's always sad now, because of Sonya. He opens the door for me.

'Thank you,' I say. My face is red.

Sonya sits next to me. We're friends again. We talk about Jeff and Andreas. 'Boys and motorbikes are the same,' she says. 'Some are exciting. Some are slow.'

2 messages

Saturday August 6th – 11.21 **by Slow Boy**

```
The girl on the bus is very shy. Her face is
always red.
```

She likes you, Slow Boy. Ask her to a café.

Monday August 8th – 6.04 **by Slow Boy**

```
I'm coming back to England soon, Junko. Let's
meet in London.
```

OK! Great!

CHAPTER 3: Slow Boy in London

Thursday August 11th – 15.47   **by Junko**

'Hi, Junko.'
'Hi, Jeff.'
'Come and talk to me.'
'First I want to …'
'What? What do you do on the computers?'
'I write emails to my family in Japan.'
'Your family? Cool.' Jeff likes touching my hand. He isn't shy.
'Come to a party with me, Junko. See you here at 8.30 on Saturday, OK?'
How can I say no? It's not polite.
'OK,' I say.
'Great. I love girls with glasses.'

0 messages

Friday August 12th – 18.19   **by Junko**

Silvio says, 'Junko, I'm going to a café with Petra and David from school. Can you come with us?'
'Yes, great. Thank you.'

It's fun with Silvio and Petra and David. We talk about cinema and sport. I'm bad at sport and Silvio is too. But he's clever and polite.

He asks me to the cinema on Saturday night with Petra and David.
But I say, 'I'm going to a party.'

He says, 'With who?'
'You don't know him.'
'Is it Jeff?'
'How do you know about Jeff?'
'From you.'
'Me? Oh? … I can't go to the cinema *and* the party.'
'Say no to the party, Junko. Come with us.'

How does Silvio know about Jeff, Internet?

0 messages

Monday August 15th – 15.38　　　　　　　　　　　**by Junko**

On Saturday night, Jeff and I go to the party on his motorbike. There are 200 people in a small room. They are dancing and drinking.

'Give me your jacket, Junko. It's hot in here. Let's have a drink.'

Jeff is dancing. He takes my hand. I dance too. But I don't like dancing. I feel very hot. It's 12.45 – very late.

Jeff says, 'Give me a kiss, baby. For fun.'
'I can't! I ... I ... I don't know the words for ...'
'Words? A kiss, baby, not words.'

He kisses me. I run into the next room. Then I remember: Sonya's number is on my mobile.

'Sonya, help me! I'm at a party. I can't get home. I haven't got a car. I'm in ... Where are we?' I ask a girl.
'Belgravia Drive in Camden.'
'We're at Belgravia Drive in Camden, Sonya. Come and find me, please.'
'OK. I love parties, Junko. See you soon.'

Today in school, Sonya says, 'Great party, Junko! I like Jeff. Andreas is nice, and he's got lots of money. But Jeff is different. He's got no money now but he's opening a second internet café. I've got his mobile number.'
'Yes, yes,' I say. But I feel sad. I can only go to the internet café at lunchtime now. Jeff isn't there at lunch.

2 messages

Monday August 15th – 15.45	by Slow Boy

```
I'm in London! Let's meet tomorrow at the
internet café.
```

At the internet café? I don't know.

Monday August 15th – 15.46	by Slow Boy

```
But lunchtime is OK. We can meet at 1 o'clock.
```

OK, at 1 o'clock. Jeff isn't in the café at lunchtime. You always remember my problems, Slow Boy!

Tuesday August 16th – 12.45 **by Junko**

In fifteen minutes, Slow Boy is arriving.

Jeff comes into the café and sits at his computer. It's lunchtime. Why is he here? I put my head down. Please don't see me, Jeff.
BING! A new message on my blog. It's from Slow Boy!

4 messages

Tuesday August 16th – 12.51 **by Slow Boy**

```
Hello Junko, I'm here in the café!
```

In the café? But there are ten boys in the café! Which of them is you, Slow Boy?

Tuesday August 16th – 12.51 **by Slow Boy**

```
Which do you think?
```

Have you got dark hair?

Tuesday August 16th – 12.53 **by Slow Boy**

```
You know me, Junko. I don't live in Tokyo.
That's only a story. I live in London.
```

A story? I know you? You mean ...

Tuesday August 16th – 12.54 **by Slow Boy**

```
Yes, that's right. You like computers. I like computers.
```

I look up. Jeff is watching me. Oh no! He smiles and gets up. Slow Boy is Jeff! Then one of the boys at the computers gets up, too. It's Silvio. He smiles. My face is red.

'Hello, Junko,' says Silvio.
'Hello, Junko,' says Jeff.

Help me, Internet! Which is Slow Boy?

FACT FILE

THE WEB WORLD

INTERNET CAFÉS

The world loves internet cafés. There are about 100,000 internet cafés in the world – 80 of them in London. How many internet cafés are there in your town?

London's Easy Internet Café has about 400 computers. But many cafés in India and China only have one or two computers. 'It's not important,' says Arun, 16, from Delhi. 'With one computer, I can talk to the world.'

'I love the internet café in my town. I play games there or surf the internet.'
Sehlu, 13, Zimbabwe

'I surf on wi-fi internet. Internet cafés are dead!'
Wayne, 15, Wales

'I shop online at an internet café. I'm not good with computers, but the people at the café help me.'
Margaret, 60, England

'Internet cafés are expensive. I surf the net at the library. You don't pay there, but you can't play computer games.'
Jacob, 13, Scotland

What do these words mean? You can look in a dictionary.
the world   to surf the net   online   a library   wi-fi

BLOGGING

Do you know?

- Blog is short for web log.

- At blogcatalog.com and other websites you can find thousands of blogs.

- 35% of British teenagers want their own blog, but usually they don't have time.

- There are bloggers in China, in Iraq, in Niger, in Sri Lanka. They tell the world about their country's problems.

'I live in Sweden, in the Arctic Circle. It's very cold. There are only 75 people in my village, and only five teenagers. It's very boring, and I've got no love life here. But I write a blog now and a girl from the next village, Katarina, writes messages to me. It's 50km to her village. I like her photo. We're meeting next Saturday for the first time.'
Lars, 17

Start a blog – it's easy. Write about your life. Or write messages to a blogger. Then the blogger can write to you.

'My blog's great. People like reading about my life after the tsunami. Things are very difficult here in Sri Lanka. My family is very poor. But I have lots of friends now in Europe and America.'
Chandrika, 16

'I love my blog. It's two today. I write for 45 minutes every day – about life in London, about my friends, my mum and dad, my school. I take photos of people on the streets and put them on my blog too.' Jane, 13

> **What do these words mean?**
> a website   my own   a circle
> a village   a tsunami

> **Do you read or write blogs? Find some on the internet. Which is your favourite?**

FACT FILE
Lonely in London

Many teenagers go and learn English in Britain. London, Brighton, Oxford and Cambridge are good places for language schools.

Students usually live with a British family. Stanny from Greece says, 'My family in Cambridge has a big house and a garden. I like their daughter. She's 27. I'm only 17, but she takes me to pubs with her friends. It's great for my English.'

But some teenagers don't talk much to their family in Britain. Sometimes the family isn't very friendly. But often the students are shy.

In London there are people from every country in the world. It's an exciting place. But people don't often stop and talk. Pascale, 16, says, 'I come from a small town in Switzerland. I know every family in the town. We sometimes talk for hours in the street. London's very different. People are always in a hurry.'

About 25% of language students never have an English friend. Angelique from France says, 'I talk to students from the school. We always use English. But it's difficult with English people. They talk very fast.'

Milos, 18, from the Czech Republic says, 'That's not true. English people are fun. Ask them and they talk slowly. I've got hundreds of friends in London.'

What do these words mean? You can look in a dictionary.

a pub   in a hurry   a group   a club

How do you make friends in Britain? Here are Milos's ideas:

1 Don't only talk to your language school friends. Talk to people in shops, in cafés, on the bus …

2 Does your British family have any teenage friends? Maybe you can meet them.

3 Go out with one friend from your language school, not lots. The English don't often talk to people in big groups.

4 Don't talk about your life. Ask questions about your new friend. Maybe you can't understand every word of his/her answers. But it's very good for your English!

5 English people love dancing. Go to a club. English music is great.

6 Find an English girlfriend / boyfriend!

> **Do people from different countries come to your town? Are the people from your town friendly to them?**

SELF-STUDY ACTIVITIES

Chapter 1

Before you read

You can use a dictionary for these activities.

1 Put these words into the sentences.
   **touch   life   blog   lonely
   messages   language school**
   a) I write a _____ . People like reading about my _____ on the internet.
   b) Don't _____ that light! It's very hot.
   c) 'Where do you have your English lessons?' 'At a _____ in London.'
   d) I'm _____ . I've got no friends in this town. But my friends from home send me email _____ every day.

2 What can you always find in an internet café?
   a) drinks   b) computers   c) motorbikes
   d) glasses e) owners

After you read

3 Answer these questions.
   a) Who is Junko living with in London?
   b) How does Junko know Sonya?
   c) Why is Junko sad in Oxford?
   d) Why don't Sonya and Silvio look at the buildings?
   e) Who does Junko talk to at the internet café?

4 What do you think?
   a) Why does Junko start a blog?
   b) Is Sonya a good friend to Junko?
   c) At the end of the story, Junko likes one of these people very much. Which one?
      i) Jeff   ii) Silvio   iii) Sonya

Chapter 2

Before you read
You can use a dictionary for these activities.

5 Put these words into the sentences on the right, so they mean the same as the sentences on the left.

slow   shy   polite   sad   expensive

a) He doesn't like meeting new people.   He's _____ .
b) It costs lots of money.   It's _____ .
c) She isn't happy.   She's _____ .
d) The train doesn't go fast.   The train is _____ .
e) He always says 'please' and 'thank you'.   He's _____ .

6 Choose the right answer.
A man says to a woman, 'Hi, baby.' He uses the word 'baby' because:
a) she's very young.
b) she's his girlfriend.
c) she's crying.

After you read
7 Are these sentences right or wrong? Change any mistakes.
a) Slow Boy is learning English.
b) Sonya likes Silvio because he's rich.
c) Junko goes on Jeff's motorbike.
d) Andreas likes motorbikes.
e) Silvio is happy because of Sonya.

8 What do you think?
a) Are motorbikes cool?
b) Is Jeff a good friend to Junko?
c) Does Junko meet Slow Boy in the next chapter? Does she like him?

SELF-STUDY ACTIVITIES

Chapter 3

Before you read

9 Put these words into the sentences.
   dancing   party   room   kiss
   a) On Saturday night I'm going to a friend's _____ .
   b) I like _____ with my boyfriend.
   c) Give me a _____ , baby.
   d) There are 100 people in the _____ .

After you read

10 Answer these questions.
   a) Who asks Junko to a party on Saturday night?
   b) Who asks her to the cinema on the same night?
   c) Why does Junko run out of the room at the party?
   d) Why does Sonya come to the party?
   e) Does Sonya like Jeff? Why/Why not?

11 Are these sentences right or wrong? Change any mistakes.
   At the end of the story:
   a) Junko doesn't go to the internet café at lunchtime.
   b) Slow Boy arrives late at the internet café.
   c) There are only two boys in the internet café.
   d) It isn't true that Slow Boy lives in Tokyo.
   e) Silvio and Jeff come and talk to Junko at the same time.

12 What do you think?
   a) Who is Slow Boy: Jeff or Silvio? Why?
   b) What happens next, to Junko, Jeff and Silvio?
   c) Can you make true friends on the internet?
   d) Are blogs interesting or boring?

Notes

Remember: be careful online. NEVER give your full name, e-mail address, home address, telephone number or other personal information.
Don't give this information to anyone online without your parents' permission.

New Words!

What do these words mean?

baby (n) …………………………..

blog (n) …………………………..

dance (v) …………………………..

glasses (n) …………………………..

kiss (n & v) …………………………..

language school (n) …………………………..

life (n) …………………………..

lonely (adj) …………………………..

message (n) …………………………..

motorbike (n) …………………………..

owner (n) …………………………..

party (n) …………………………..

polite (adj) …………………………..

shy (adj) …………………………..

touch (v) …………………………..